CONTENTS MAP

Section	Page
FC Writing: an overview	page 2
Unit sections	page 2
FC writing skills	page 3
Composition marking	page 5
FCE Paper 2 – Writing: Marking	page 6
Lesson notes and answer key (Units 1–28)	pages 7–25

First Certificate Writing: an overview

The rationale behind this book is to provide a highly exam-focused set of materials that are transparent to both teachers and students, which can be covered comfortably within one teaching year, and which train students in the writing skills necessary to cope with the requirements of the Cambridge First Certificate In English, Paper 2.

However, the book can also be used flexibly as supplementary material, and dipped into whenever the teacher identifies the need for further work on specific text types.

Each unit of the book identifies a text type as a starting point, and these text types are to be found as unit titles. Furthermore, each unit title focuses on the most frequent text types occurring in the examination, researched extensively from past papers. The start of every unit is always an exam question, also based closely on UCLES questions from past papers.

The scheme of work for each unit is to take learners through

a   an analysis and awareness-raising stage, followed by

b   a controlled practice stage, followed by

c   a writing task with guidelines

d   a writing task which allows learners to write independently without any guidance at all.

Unit sections

Read the question

This section asks students to analyse the question by identifying key words. This will help to highlight the aspects of the topic that should be covered, and the type of text required. In some early units, the tasks include questions to direct students to the relevant parts of the question. In later units, the task simply instructs students to underline the key words. This is always the first task in every unit, and serves to develop this analysis as a natural habit in students when faced with an examination question. It also emphasises the fact that the questions must be answered fully to pass.

Think about your reader

This section aims to focus students sharply on who is going to read the piece of writing. The examination has been carefully designed to provide realistic writing tasks for a variety of readers. The examiner/teacher reading the answer will have to place herself or himself in the shoes of the target reader, and judge if the answer is appropriate.

In order to train students to evaluate the effect the target reader has on the way the answer is written, this section of each unit also provides questions to help students decide on aspects of style and content.

Brainstorm the topic

Many topics included in the examination are familiar to students, but there are also some that may be less so. Even if the topic is familiar, students may have trouble

getting started because they find it hard to assemble enough ideas, especially in a limited time, in class or in the exam. This section asks students to discuss questions in pairs or groups to focus on the topic and relevant ideas for inclusion in the composition. During the discussion, students should be encouraged to take notes, so that they can later select the best ideas to use.

Read a model text / Think about paragraphing

Each unit contains a 'model' answer of some kind. In the early units, only 'good' models are provided. In later units, 'poor' models are also provided for students to evaluate through a checklist based on the main areas found in the UCLES assessment criteria. Some units provide two models for comparison and evaluation.

Each model answer has associated tasks, which focus students on various aspects of text construction, such as paragraph structure, relevance of ideas, sequencing of ideas, and so on. Students are often asked to make an outline from the model, so that they can develop their own organisational skills. Students are introduced to different ways to outline an answer, (mind maps, tables, flowcharts, numbered notes) and should be encouraged to choose a method which suits them individually.

Think about topic sentences

This section appears in the earlier units of the book, and is concerned with giving students an overview of how a paragraph is structured. From this foundation, students will learn how to present new information to the reader in a clearly signalled way, with a general statement providing the focus for a paragraph (the topic sentence), followed by relevant supporting details.

Link your text

This section focuses on the use of cohesive devices used to connect ideas in a text. The tasks deal with simple co-ordinating conjunctions (and, but, so, etc.), subordinate clauses (relative, concessive etc.), adverbial conjunctions (However, Therefore, In addition, etc.), as well as discourse markers showing attitude and opinion (In my opinion, Unfortunately, To make matters worse, etc.). Once again, the selection of cohesive devices is based on the needs dictated by the question used in the unit.

Think about vocabulary

Each unit contains a section on the vocabulary needed to answer the question. Vocabulary tasks may also focus on word formation (for example, making nouns from adjectives), and also on common vocabulary errors.

Think about grammar

This section in each unit is designed to focus on the most useful language points arising from the question at the beginning of each unit, so that grammatical and functional items are covered according to the needs of the context of writing. These sections revise language the students are assumed to know. In addition, exercises focusing on error correction are included.

Be your own examiner

This is an evaluation task for students to judge how good a piece of writing is, in terms of the assessment criteria used by UCLES – see page 00 in this book for the criteria table. It is vital that students not only learn how to write, but also how to form judgements on the quality of their writing. This enables them to form a clear concept of the qualities required to succeed as writers.

Exam practice

In each unit, a second writing task, again based closely on UCLES questions, is provided towards the end of the unit. A brief checklist is usually provided to guide students to answer the question. This is the part of the unit where the teacher can see if the detailed work done up to this point in the unit can be put into practice by the students with a different answer of the same text type.

Further practice

At the end of each unit, another question is provided of the same text type with no guidance at all, for the students to work independently. This question can be set as the homework for the unit, or be used in class. If used in class, the students can work in groups to brainstorm, plan and write an essay. The final product can then be passed to another group for evaluation with a checklist. This question can also be used as a kind of 'mock' test, with a time limit, to give students the experience of writing under examination conditions.

FC writing skills

Skills and requirements

In the FCE examination, students will be tested on:

- their ability to identify from the question, and write different **text types**;
- their ability to identify from the question the **purpose** of writing, and to write according to this purpose;
- their ability to identify from the question the **target reader**, and to write appropriately for such a reader;
- their ability to handle a given **topic**.

In order for students to meet these demands, they have to demonstrate control of a number of writing 'sub-skills':

- to analyse the key elements of the question;
- to generate ideas on the given topic;
- to choose a style and level of formality which is suited to the target reader, and the purpose for writing;
- to generate related vocabulary;
- to create an organised outline or plan for the final piece of writing;
- to organise ideas into appropriate paragraphs;
- to sequence paragraphs logically;
- to write an informative, yet succinct introduction;
- to write a meaningful and satisfactory conclusion;
- to evaluate the piece of writing and revise it.

These are matters of **content**, that is, presenting ideas so that the writer's message, or intended meaning, is communicated in a way that would be relevant and meaningful, and have a positive effect on the target reader. In addition, the writer must have some control over the language with which the ideas are communicated, and these are matters of **accuracy** and **clarity**. Students must:

a write grammatically accurate text, with as much freedom from error as can be expected at the level.

b sequence words to form syntactically correct text. The word order should be as natural as can be expected at the level.

c use cohesive devices, such as connecting words (or, 'linkers') to signal 'stages' in the text, which make reading easier. These devices can be seen as the writer's signals to a reader of how the information is organised.

d determine the appropriate format for the text. A letter is set out in a fairly standard format. A report also has a certain characteristic presentation, with headings and numbered points.

e use punctuation to segment the text, and clarify meaning.

f spell words correctly.

g use handwriting that is more or less legible. Teachers should be at pains to stress that, under exam conditions, untidiness and poor handwriting are tolerated, but the latter can make a poor impression on examiners, who may have to struggle to decipher the handwriting, and the impact of the content may be diminished.

h evaluate the accuracy of the piece of writing, and edit it where corrections are needed.

The writing process

The writing process can be seen in a simple way as follows:

Analysis
↓
Brainstorming
↓
Organising
↓
Drafting
↓
Revising & editing
↓
Final version

Responding to writing

By far the most important stage in the process is how the teacher marks, or rather, responds to writing. For this reason, I believe that a 'training approach' is necessary, rather than a 'testing approach'. A testing approach involves setting students a large number of compositions, and then simply marking them. Students take one look at the grade and may never look at the piece of work again. The problem with this approach is that, while students are getting plenty of exposure to writing, they are not able to see their strengths and weaknesses easily, and cannot develop in the required direction.

A training approach, however, would allow for the writing of a composition to be a more extended and interactive exercise, with the students writing a first draft, which is then handed to the teacher for a response. The teacher then responds to matters of content and accuracy, and without grading, hands the piece of writing back to the student for revision and editing. The teacher's feedback is probably the most crucial stage in the writing process, and should be positive, encouraging and explicit, in order for students to see clearly how they should improve.

Principles and techniques for Teachers

Some suggestions for teachers teaching writing skills:

1 Always read the composition through (without a pen in your hand!) to form an overall impression, based on the UCLES assessment scheme – see page 6.

2 Start reading again, and focus your attention on content matters. Use the UCLES marking scheme and add comments to the text in the margins, or over the relevant section, or use numbers on the text, which refer to footnotes.

3 Now mark the most important errors with a code.

4 Write overall, summarising comments at the end of the composition. Be careful to respond to the message (i.e. the ideas used) on a personal level. (e.g. "I really enjoyed this description.") In addition, always find

something positive to say first. This may be hard with a very poor effort, but every piece of writing shows some kind of strength. It is also important to make comments on progress made, so that even if a composition is still not of pass standard, you can comment on areas that have been improved, no matter how small that improvement may be! Then, make comments on the areas that need improving in the second draft. It is best to avoid the word 'weakness' in teacher responses. When students hand in a revised version for grading, make sure that you get the first draft as well, to see how much progress they have made from first to final draft. Part of the final grade should reflect the amount of successful revision.

As the time for the examination approaches, drop the first draft. Students will not get this chance in the exam, and they should start getting used to one draft only. By this time, however, it is hoped that the training approach implicit in the redrafting process will have developed students' writing enough to cope with revising and editing in an examination.

It is important that students have a copy of the assessment scheme used by teachers to grade their work. In this way, both teachers and students are aware of the criteria used, and students, in addition, may begin to use the scheme as a kind of checklist for their drafts. It seems sensible that all final grades should be awarded in accordance with the published UCLES overall assessment scheme.

Composition marking

Sample marked text

The following is a sample student composition in answer to the following question (see FC Writing Students' Book, page 108, exercise 1.)

You have seen this advertisement in a newspaper:

International Students' Magazine

We arc looking for articles on favourite TV programmes around the world. Write an article, answering these questions:
- What's your favourite programme?
- Why do you like it?

The best articles will be published in next month's magazine.

Write your **article** for *International Students' Magazine* (120–180 words).

Suggested correction code

WW	Wrong word
WF	Correct word, but change the form
SP	Spelling error
P	Punctuation error
T	Tense error
WO	Word order is wrong
X	In this line, cross out one word
∧	Something is missing here

My favourite television programme is 'Floyd on Food', where

you can watch a famous cook <u>do</u> [WW] all kinds of dishes in front of   ✔ good introduction

the camera. It may not <u>seems</u> [WF] to be very interesting, but I will

✗ ✗ ✗ explain you what a good pro<u>grammes</u> [WF] this makes to people.

✗ Most of us <u>doesn't</u> [WF] like to cook and usually <u>buys</u> [WF] the junk food

✗ which it is easy to eat and very fast. I h<u>ave been</u> [T] one of those

before I watched this programme. Mr Floyd teaches us how to

make even <u>exotique</u> [SP] foods from <u>strange</u> [WW] countries and what's   ✔ good

more, he makes it look easy. You can write to the programme

and get the <u>receipt</u> [WW] if you want to make it yourself at home

without too much difficul<u>ties</u> [WF]. I <u>appreciate</u> [WW] this programme

because ∧ persuades us who don't like cook to go in our kitchen   ✔ good, well-expressed

and enjoy the experience.

✔ Organisation

✔ Clear ideas; I have a good idea about the programme.

? You could add a conclusion

? Try to write a little more — you have about 140 words — write about 180 words altogether

? You could use more connecting words

FCE Paper 2 – Writing: Marking

Marking criteria

The table below is based on the marking criteria for Paper 2 of the First Certificate Examination by the University of Cambridge Local Examinations Syndicate.

Band 5	Full realisation of task set shown by: • Coverage of points required with evidence of original input. • Wide range of structure and vocabulary demonstrating control of language. • Clear organisation with a variety of linking devices. • Presentation and register wholly appropriate to purpose and audience throughout. *Overall: a very positive effect on the target reader.*
Band 4	Good realisation of task set shown by: • Coverage of points required with sufficient detail. • Good range of structure and vocabulary; generally accurate • Effective organisation; suitable linking devices. • Presentation and register appropriate to purpose and audience. *Overall: a positive effect on the target reader.*
Band 3	Task set is reasonably achieved by: • Coverage of main points required. • Adequate range of structure and vocabulary; some errors. • Adequate organisation; simple linking devices • Presentation and register on the whole appropriate to purpose and audience. *Overall: a satisfactory effect on the target reader*
Band 2	Task set attempted but not adequately achieved because of : • Some omissions and/or irrelevant material. • Range of structure and vocabulary rather limited; errors may obscure communication. • Inconsistent organisation; few linking devices. • Unsuccessful attempts at appropriate presentation and register. *Overall: message not clearly communicated to target reader.*
Band 1	Task set not achieved because of: • Notable omissions and/or considerable irrelevance. • Narrow range of vocabulary and structure; little or no language control. • Little or no awareness of appropriate presentation and register. *Overall: a very negative effect on the target reader.*
Band 0	Too little language for assessment

Marking scheme explained

This is a banded criterion-referenced marking scheme, so all criteria stated in Band 5 apply to all the bands, but at a progressively lower level each time. Band 0 is almost never used, and is reserved for those exam papers that are not complete enough to assess.

Realisation of task through 4 main criteria:

1 **Coverage** of points required.
   This involves writing material relevant to the question as well as including all the points required by the question. This criterion is entirely concerned with the content of the answer.

2 **Wide range** of grammatical structure, **wide range** of vocabulary, **control** (i.e. accuracy) of grammatical structure, **control** of vocabulary.
   In this one criteria, both range and accuracy of both grammar and vocabulary are assessed. This effectively shows the relative importance of these issues in

answers. We can assume that grammatical accuracy, for example, is worth one quarter of one criterion.

3 **Clear organisation** with a variety of linking devices. This criterion includes paragraph organisation, with a topic sentence when needed, and relevant supporting details, relating to one clear topic per paragraph. Paragraphs should also be in a logical order, and the use of a variety of connectors within and across paragraphs is assessed.

4 **Presentation and register** appropriate to **purpose** and **audience**.
   This criterion is concerned with the appropriate format (letters and reports have a distinctive presentation format) and with the selection of the appropriate tone and style according to the purpose for writing, and target reader.

Overall effect

The answer should also be assessed on an **overall** effect, as well as the more analytical criteria above.

Informal letters

Making contact and giving news

1 Read the question

Make sure that students underline the target reader, the main topic, the text type, and the purpose for writing each time they look at a question.

1 In an English-speaking country
2 Studying
3 A friend
4 One topic (the school), two different aspects
5 c

2 Think about your reader

This section can be done quite quickly in each unit. Get students to focus on the question again, and make the point that writing for the reader is an important assessment criterion.

1 a; 2 c; 3 b; 4 b

3 Brainstorm the topic

Get learners to discuss in pairs or groups and make notes on their own ideas. The Vocabulary section which follows will add to and organise the students' vocabulary on the same topics.

4 Think about vocabulary

a Students should first put their brainstorming ideas into the table, and then complete the table with the words in **b**.

b **Building/Classrooms**
Positive: brightly decorated, spacious
Negative: cramped, depressing, gloomy, noisy

Classmates
Positive: friendly, fun, funny, helpful, interesting, kind,
Negative: boring, noisy

Teachers
Positive: encouraging, helpful, kind, interesting, friendly, fun, funny, motivating, well organised, stimulating
Negative: disorganised, boring, strict, demanding

Lessons
Positive: interesting, fun, helpful, motivating, stimulating, well organised
Negative: boring, disorganised, long, noisy

Facilities
Positive: well organised, helpful,
Negative: disorganised,

Location
Positive: spacious
Negative: gloomy, noisy

5 Think about your introduction

a Students should underline 'How are you?' Look at the Writing Bank, and/or elicit other greetings.

b Olga also gives recent news about her busy time getting ready to go to England.

c **Suggested answers**
1 'Thanks for your long letter. It was really great to hear all your news, after not hearing from you for ages. Congratulations on passing your driving test!'
2 'How are things with you? I'm sorry I haven't written for so long, but I have been taking some very important exams at school, and I have had to stay up late studying every night for the past month! I'm glad it's all over now, so that I can finally reply to your last letter.'

6 Think about paragraphing

Extract 2 is easier to read, because it has put positive ideas in one paragraph, and negative ideas in the other. Extract 1 mixes the topics and has no paragraphs.

7 Read a model text

Paragraph 2: d, b, f
Paragraph 3: c, e, a, g

8 Think about your conclusion

a Olga invites Anna to visit her and asks her to write back.

b 1 1 sending; 2 write; 3 tell; 4 news
   2 1 give/send; 2 parents, brother, etc; 3 write; 4 next summer, the holidays, etc.
   3 1 like, love; 2 come; 3 soon, back soon

9 Think about language

1 I'm sorry <u>I haven't written</u> ...
2 I'm very <u>interested</u> ...
3 I'm looking forward to <u>seeing</u> ...
4 Please <u>tell me</u> ..
5 ... when I <u>arrive</u>. ...
6 ... what <u>did you see</u> there?
7 <u>I have been waiting</u> to ...
8 I arrived <u>in</u> London ...

Exam practice

Get students to look at the checklist questions, and make a plan for the composition. This can be done in pairs or groups. The writing of the composition can be done individually, or as a co-operative effort. Students can exchange papers to edit each other's work for errors. An alternative is to discuss the planning in class, and then students can do the writing for homework. Peer editing can be done in the next lesson, if desired.

Further practice

The same procedure can be followed as in *Exam practice*, or this section can be used as a progress test for the unit.

Informal letters

2 Giving advice

1 Read the question

1 a reply
2 Where to go and what to pack

2 Think about your reader

1 An English pen friend
2 a, b
3 b, d

4 Think about vocabulary

b 1 raincoat; 2 scarf; 3 sweater; 4 boots; 5 gloves;
6 skis; 7 swimsuit; 8 sandals; 9 sunglasses;
10 trainers; 11 snorkel and mask; 12 shorts

5 Read a model text

The answer includes a, b, e.

6 Think about paragraphing

a 4 paragraphs
b Paragraph 1: b

Paragraph 2: c, g, h

Paragraph 3: e, i

Paragraph 4: a, d, f

c This is the chance for students to use their personal knowledge to write. This can be done in pairs/groups to generate ideas for the notes.

d Students should use the model outline in b, and transfer their notes to an organised format.

7 Think about topic sentences

b 1 *Topic sentence* – 'The West coast of Scotland is a wonderful place.' *4 details* – beaches, sunsets, scenery, people

2 *Topic sentence* – 'You asked me what you should pack.' *3 details* – clothes, weather, camera

c Students can now look back at their outline they made in **6d**, and write topic sentences for each paragraph. They can also look at the details they have for each paragraph. Once the topic sentence has been written, they may need to add more details to the outline.

8 Think about language

b **Suggested answers**
1 If I were you, I'd bring plenty of suntan lotion, as the sun is very strong.

2 You should avoid Mykonos, because it's very crowded and expensive.

3 If you want a good restaurant, try Chez Michel.

4 If I were you, I'd stay in a guest house, as they are very clean and good value for money.

5 If you want an exciting nightlife, don't forget to go to the Club Copacabana.

6 If you want to see all the coastline, you should hire a boat.

7 You shouldn't visit in August, because the weather is too hot.

8 If I were you, I'd travel by taxi, because the buses are too slow and unreliable.

Informal letters

3 Describing an object

1 Read the question

1 A reply
2 A new stereo or a new computer
3 a, c, e,
4 your other news

2 Think about your reader

b

4 Think about vocabulary

Car	economical, high-tech, luxurious, reliable, roomy, smart, stylish, upmarket,
TV	bulky, high-tech, portable, smart, state-of-the-art, upmarket
Stereo	bulky, compact, efficient, high-tech, portable, smart, state-of-the-art, upmarket
Bicycle	compact, smart,
Motorbike	economical, reliable, smart, stylish, upmarket
Computer	bulky, compact, efficient, high-tech, portable, smart, state-of-the-art, user friendly
Trainers	fashionable, roomy, smart, stylish, trendy, upmarket
Watch	bulky, fashionable, high-tech, smart, state-of-the-art, stylish, trendy, upmarket

b Students should write about two or three of their own possessions. The order of adjectives may need to be revised – see the **Writing Bank**, *FC Writing* Students' Book page 124.

5 Read a model text

a No. The topics are mixed up in the two main body paragraphs.

b *Topic sentences*:
1 Thanks for your letter.
2 Now for my news.
3 I finally decided on a computer rather than a stereo.
4 That's all for now

c *Underline*: I went on a short trip ... rearranging my room. + I also went to a beach party ... midnight!

d *Circle*: It also makes writing ... change anything I write. + It's a portable, compact notebook ... just about anywhere!

e Once students have managed to sort out the mixed topics, they should have the table completed in an organised fashion. It is then a simple matter of writing out the letter from the table outline. Students can also be encouraged to add linking or connecting words, and think about the order of the details. (e.g. in paragraph 3, the description of the computer may be better immediately after the topic sentence.)

6 Think about connectors

a a) reason – because, as,
b) result – so, as a result

b Suggested answers

1 I bought a new stereo, as my old one was beyond repair.

2 I went to my grandmother's house, because I hadn't seen her for ages.

3 I decided to buy a computer; as a result, I finished my homework in half the time.

4 I watched TV all night, so I was too tired to do well in my exam.

5 I spent hours on the Internet; as a result, my phone bill was huge!

6 I bought a new bicycle, because I couldn't stand travelling by bus.

7 Think about tenses

a *Underline*: haven't written, has made, went, enjoy, found, had bought, went,

b **1** d; **2** d; **3** c; **4** b; **5** c, a; **6** c

Formal letters

 A letter of application

2 Think about your reader

1 No; **2** No; **3** business; **4** a, b, c, f, h, i; **5** a

3 Brainstorm the topic

1 *Other possibilities*: housewives with children at school, someone with another part-time job, a high school student wanting a summer job, etc.

2 *Other possibilities*: good knowledge of local tourist attractions, travel routes, accommodation, etc. Good telephone skills.

3 *Other possibilities*: organised, calm, outgoing, polite, a good listener, understanding, etc.

4 Compare two model texts

a **1** B; **2** Letter A uses contractions, B uses full verb forms; **3** A; **4** B; **5** A

b B

5 Think about style

a *Underline*:

1 'I am writing to apply for the job ... *Daily News*.'

2 '... and would like the opportunity to practise my languages with foreigners.'

3 'I also speak some Italian.'

4 'I worked as a tourist guide last summer, with Blue Sky Holidays, which I enjoyed very much.'

5 '... I would say that I have a good knowledge of ...'

6 'I can be contacted at the above address ... your reply.'

7 'Yours Faithfully, Simon Garrett.'

b **1** completed; **2** opportunity; **3** gain; **4** valuable; **5** considering; **6** I have a good knowledge of; **7** I can be contacted; **8** I look forward to your reply.

c **1** received; **2** enjoyable; **3** was impressed by; **4** fluently; **5** I am willing to work; **6** I am available for work; **7** attend; **8** considerable

6 Think about paragraphing

Paragraph	Main Topic	Details
1	Purpose for writing	information officer, Daily News
2	Why interested in job	help with studies, experience, career
3	Previous experience	like people, guide, knowledge
4	Conclusion	contact details

7 Think about grammar

a In the first sentence, **which** refers to 'job'. In the second, **which** refers to the whole of the first clause.

b 1 I went to America last summer, where I improved my English a lot.

2 I worked with Mr. Andrews, who taught me how to use a computer.

3 I am studying French, which I enjoy very much.

4 I enclose the names of two people who can give you references for me.

5 I work in an office where there are many foreign visitors.

Formal letters

5 Making a request

1 Read the question

b, d

2 Think about your reader

1 Mr. Wilson; **2** c; **3** c; **4** c, or possibly a, if a good relationship was established.

3 Brainstorm the topic

This is an exercise in visualisation. If students do not have their own experiences to draw upon for ideas, then they need to exercise their imagination. Get students to close their eyes, and build up a realistic picture of the people and objects in the situation. For the character of Mr. Wilson, ask the students to describe him – *How old is he? What colour hair? Married? Personality?* and so on. An alternative is to bring in magazine pictures of different people, and ask students to choose which 'picture' they would like to write to.

4 Read a model text

Yes, the greeting and ending are appropriate, and so is the style.

5 Think about paragraphing

Paragraph	Topic sentence	Details
1 Introduction	I am writing to thank you very much for making my stay so enjoyable.	advice, fruit
2 Request to find glasses	I wonder if I could ask you a favour.	glasses – gold frames, red plastic case, restaurant
3 Request to post	If you manage to find ... home address?	registered mail, pay for postage, how much? cheque
4 Conclusion		contact if problems, thanks

6 Think about topic sentences

a **1** b; **2** a; **3** c

b This is an open-ended task, so spend some time discussing what details would be appropriate before students write.

Suggested answer for 1
The holiday brochures are very helpful, and the map will be very useful for me when I get there.

c **Suggested answers**
1 I am writing to thank you very much for making my trip so pleasant.

2 Unfortunately, when I got home, I realised that I had left my pen behind.

3 Luckily, my sister/mother/friend is going to London next month.

7 Think about vocabulary

1 Thank you for your generosity in spending so much time with me.

2 Thank you for your helpfulness when I needed to know something.

3 Thank you for your hospitality during my stay in your hotel.

4 Thank you for your patience with my terrible English!

5 Thank you for your efficiency in sending me the brochure so quickly.

6 Thank you for your encouragement when I tried to speak English.

7 Thank you for your co-operation when I had to change my hotel booking.

8 Thank you for your sympathy when I received the bad news.

8 Think about language

a *Underline*:
- could you please ...
- Would it be possible for you to ...
- I would be very grateful if you could ...

The verb form used is the past conditional.

b **Suggested answers**
1 Could you please arrange for a taxi to meet me at the airport?

2 Would it be possible for you to give me a lift to the station?

3 Could you please tell me how much it will cost?

4 Would it be possible for you to look for my jacket?

5 I would be very grateful if you could send me some information about your school.

Formal letters

6 A letter to the editor

1 Read the question

1 Traffic in city centres; **2** Traffic must be kept out of city centres; **3** b, and maybe a, as supporting details

2 Think about your reader

1 The editor, and the reading public
2 Dear Sir, Yours faithfully
3 Formal

3 Think about vocabulary

Vehicles: bus, coach, lorry, motorbike, van
Problems: air pollution, asthma, exhaust fumes, noise pollution, the rush hour, traffic jam,

Fuel: diesel, unleaded petrol
Places to drive/walk: bypass, crossroads, junction, motorway, pavement,
Parking: car park, to park
Adjectives: crowded, filthy, frustrating, noisy, smelly,
People: cyclist, driver, pedestrian,

b

Adjective	Can describe:
Frustrating	traffic jams, the rush hour,
Filthy	exhaust fumes, air pollution,
Smelly	exhaust fumes, air pollution, lorries
Crowded	motorways, pavements, bus, car park
Noisy	lorry, the rush hour

5 Read a model text

1 The writer agrees with the letter.
2 Formal

6 Think about paragraphing

a 5
b (The ideas already on the ideas map are in brackets below)

Paragraph 2: *Pollution* – health improved – *trees and plants*

Paragraph 3: *Effects on people* – tired, frustrated – traffic jams – *public transport and walking*

Paragraph 4: *Parking* – cars on pavements – pedestrians in road – safe shopping

7 Think about language

a *Underline*:
- I believe
- I am strongly in favour of
- I think

b **2** I do not agree/I disagree
3 I am strongly against
4 It's wonderful/good/etc.

8 Think about your introduction

Encourage students to discuss their opinions, and then write an introduction, using the language in 7.

Suggested answer for 1

I have read a letter in your newspaper about the lack of a recycling scheme in our town. I completely agree with the writer – our council should do something about this immediately.

9 Think about grammar

a No
b *Underline*:
were banned, would not be, would flourish, were, would use, would be

10 Think about connectors

a *Underline*:
'Firstly, we have … in our city.', 'Furthermore, many people … work.', 'Finally, parking … in the road.'

b *Circle*:
Firstly, Furthermore, Finally

Transactional letters
7 Asking for information

1 Read the question

a The differences are that there is an extended input text, which contains points that must be used in the answer.
b 1, 2, 4, 5, 7, 8, 9, 11,

2 Think about your reader

a **Informal letters**: Dear, Best wishes, Love
Formal letters: Dear, Yours sincerely, Dear Sir/Madam, Yours faithfully,
b Dear Sir/ Madam, Yours faithfully
Formal

3 Think about vocabulary

Places to stay: bed & breakfast, campsite, caravan, guest house, top-class hotel,

Hotel facilities: beauty salon, gym, lift, room service, sauna, tennis court

Summer activities: buying souvenirs, diving, sailing, sightseeing, sunbathing, surfing,

Winter activities: buying souvenirs, sightseeing, skating, skiing, snowboarding

4 Read a model text

a Yes
b family size, length of stay, two children,
c

Paragraph	Main Topic	Details
2	Booking and prices	2 weeks, Aug. or Oct. family of 4, prices, 2 small children – babysitting
3	More information – chalets	No. of bedrooms? restaurant? nearest town?
4	Sports	Which ones? Prices?

5 Think about paragraphing

a This is best done as a discussion activity. There are 10 points to be sorted into paragraphs, and ordered. Many different versions are possible.

Suggested answer
8 belongs in the introduction
Paragraph 2 could be about the school itself – 5, 7, 9, 3
Paragraph 3 could be about accommodation – 4, 10
Paragraph 4 could be about money – 1, 2, 6

b Once decisions have been made in **a**, get students to make an outline as in **4c** above (or any other format for an outline that the students prefer.)

6 Think about your introduction

a *Underline*:

'With reference to your advertisement in ...',
'I am writing to ...'

b **Suggested answers**

1 With reference to your advertisement in the *Daily Telegraph*, I am writing to ask for more information about your furnished flat in Paris.

2 With reference to your advertisement in the *Independent*, I am writing to enquire about your short stay apartments in London.

7 Think about grammar

a 1 Do you have any vacancies in early August or early October?

2 Could you tell me the price for two small chalets?

3 How many bedrooms does the large chalet have?

b A direct question must use an auxiliary verb, or invert the subject and verb.

An indirect question uses the syntax for a normal statement.

c **Suggested answers**

1 I would like to know if you have a swimming pool.

2 Could you tell me how much a double room costs?

3 Could you tell me if there are any vacancies in June?

4 I would be very grateful if you could tell me how far the airport is from the hotel.

5 I would like to know if you organise sightseeing trips.

6 Could you tell me if there are any shops nearby?

7 I would be grateful if you could tell me which bus goes from the airport to the hotel.

8 I would like to know if all the rooms have a view of the sea.

Transactional letters

 Giving information

1 Read the question

Most transactional letters have a lot of input text to read. It helps students to understand that the input is usually divided into: situation, reading matter, and writing instructions

- **information about the situation**: The first four sentences: 'You are ... travel agent.'
- **what you have to read**: the travel options, the timetables, and the prices in the boxes below the question.
- **what you have to write**: a letter, giving information about the three ways to travel, suggest the best way, explain why.
- **need to summarise**: the travel methods, times and prices

2 Think about your reader

1 *Underline*: 'two English-speaking friends living in your country.'

2 Informal

3 Brainstorm the topic

a 1 Train = 3 hours 35 mins., coach = 6 hours, 15 mins. Car will be much faster than the coach, and slightly faster than the train.

2 Coach

3 Coach

4 b

b 1 by coach on a weekday; 2 afternoon; 3 evening; 4 morning; 5 expensive/£60, and £75 at weekends; 6 expensive/over £70; 7 faster

4 Read a model text

b, e, c, a, g, f, d

5 Think about paragraphing

a *Underline*:

'First of all,'; 'Another option is to ...' 'The final choice is ...'

b Get the students to write each topic sentence in a table or an ideas web. Then they can easily add the details for the task in **c**.

Suggested answer to 1:
The first way is to take the ferry.
Another option is to fly.
The last possibility is to drive.

c Students will produce a complete letter here. Get them to add details in their outline in pairs or groups. Then students can write the complete letter, adding an introduction and conclusion.

6 Think about vocabulary

1 The journey/trip to Scotland ... 'Travel' can only be a verb, not a noun.

2 I'm very excited ... When writing about your own feelings, use '-ed'. When talking about other people or things seem to you, use '-ing.'

3 I've got all the information ... 'Information' is an uncountable noun.

4 There is a big car park ... 'Parking' is a gerund, or part of a verb tense.

5 ... so we had to stay at a campsite. 'Camping' is a gerund, or part of a verb tense.

6 Accommodation in the city ... 'Accommodation' is an uncountable noun.

7 ... because of the high cost. 'Cost' can be described as 'high' or 'low'.

8 ... all kinds of entertainment. 'Entertainment' is an uncountable noun.

9 My favourite way to travel / The way I prefer to travel is by plane. 'Most preferred' doesn't exist in English!

10 I've made many trips to New York. 'Trip' needs the verb 'make', not 'do'.

7 Think about grammar

a The first conditional with the present simple:
If + present simple, will + infinitive

Transactional letters

 Giving & asking for information

1 Read the question

a *Give information*: yourself, how much you know, what you want to improve, why you want to improve

Ask for information: price, time, place, class size, books

b Accept any close guesses.
The exact meaning is 'improve', or 'review knowledge'.

2 Think about your reader

1 Carol McBride

2 Fairly formal

3 Probably only: age, where you study/work

4 Compare two model texts

a Text A

b *Writing checklist*:

1 A Yes, B Yes, but information is not well organised, and information asked for reads like an abrupt series of direct questions.

2 A Yes, B No

3 A Yes, B No – style is rather abrupt and too direct. More polite expressions are needed. Over familiar – 'That's all for now.'; 'Phone me.';

4 A Yes, B No— The introduction is too abrupt, and purpose for writing is not stated.

5 A Yes, B No

6 A Yes, B No

7 A Yes, B No

8 A Yes, B No

5 Think about language

a Get students to think of as many ways as possible to write questions on one topic, to show them the need for variety in their writing.

6 Edit your text

I have seen your advertisement about English lessons. I would like to <u>give you</u> some <u>information</u> about myself, and <u>ask you</u> some questions I have. I am a <u>17-year-old</u> student at secondary school. I would like to improve my English because I am <u>interested</u> in doing a job in the tourist business. I <u>have been learning</u> English for three years in a private school. I am good at grammar, but I have difficulty <u>in writing</u> very <u>well</u>. I would like to have lessons in writing essays. I <u>would be</u> grateful if you could <u>tell me</u> some things about your lessons. I would like to know how much <u>they cost</u>. Where <u>do you give</u> the lessons? Could you tell me how many students <u>you have</u> in your classes? Can I have lessons <u>by myself/on my own</u>? Please <u>call me/give me a ring/give me a call/ telephone me</u> (567-992).
I look forward to <u>hearing</u> from you.

Transactional letters

 Making arrangements

1 Read the question

b *Tell*:

- Fri. 3rd. or Sat. 4th.; time – 8.00pm Fri. or 11.00am, Sat.
- subject of talk – 'How British teenagers spend their free time'
- transport – taxi to hotel, and then to school

Ask:

- which day she prefers
- please bring photos.

2 Think about your reader

1 Stella Brown. She is someone you have never met, a friend of your teacher's. She is also likely to be older than you.

2 Formal, but friendly

3 Dear Ms. Brown, … Yours Sincerely, (full name)

3 Make a plan

a This is an exercise in making an ideas web. The first stage is to simply put all the required information onto the diagram.

b This is the organising stage. When students have decided what goes in each paragraph, use one colour to highlight each paragraph idea.

c The final stage is to order the paragraphs. Number each colour in order.

4 Compare two model texts

a B

b *Writing checklist*:

1 A Yes, B Yes, but it is very disorganised

2 A No, B Yes

3 A Yes, B No

4 A Yes, B No

5 A Yes, B No

c • 'Maybe I can tell you the best places for sightseeing.'

- '… bring photos of popular places for tourists to visit in your town.'
- 'They like sports and going to the cinema.'

d • Dear Stella

- Thanks a lot
- Maybe
- Now about the talk
- kids
- I mean,
- If it's OK with you
- we want
- We're all crazy about the idea
- + all contracted verb forms

5 Think about your introduction

a for + -ing

b Suggested answer to 1

Thank you very much for sending me all those wonderful posters. They will certainly make our school look colourful, and give our students an idea about Britain and its culture at the same time.

6 Think about your conclusion

b Suggested answers:

1 would like; **2** get in touch with/contact; **3** phone number; **4** will call; **5** confirm; **6** are; **7** looking forward

7 Think about prepositions

1 for; **2** to; **3** at; **4** at; **5** on; **6** for; **7** to; **8** about; **9** into; **10** at; **11** in; **12** for; **13** to; **14** to

8 Think about grammar

b **1** to do; **2** not to go; **3** driving; **4** to stop; **5** spending; **6** to meet; **7** finding; **8** of spending; **9** for inviting; **10** about coming

Transactional letters

 Making a complaint

2 Think about your reader

a 1 An employee of City World Tours. Dear Sir/Madam, Yours faithfully

   2 Formal

b 1 Too strong and threatening. This would not get a good response.

   2 Not strong enough. Complaints must be polite but direct.

   3 Appropriate. Notice the request is polite, ('I would like ...',) but gets straight to the point.

4 Read a model text

All the points are appropriately dealt with in the letter.

5 Link your text

a *Underline*:

Even though, To make matters worse, Furthermore, However, despite, In addition, and

b *Contrast*: Even though, However, despite,

   Addition: To make matters worse, Furthermore, In addition, and

c **Suggested answers**

- The air conditioner in my room was broken, and despite my three requests for it to be repaired, nothing was done.

- In addition, I paid for a tour. However, the tour guide was sick, and no replacement guide was found.

- Even though your advertisement stated that all rooms had a view of the sea, mine had a view of the car park and dustbins. Furthermore, I couldn't

open the window because of the smell from the dustbins.

- I couldn't sleep all night because of the noise from the hotel night club. In addition, the bed was hard, and the toilet was broken.

- The receptionist was rude, and the waiters were very offhand. To make matters worse, my room was not cleaned at all during my stay.

7 Think about your introduction

a The information included in the introductions is:

- Reason for writing (to make a complaint),

- Background to the complaint; where, when it happened, where advertisement was seen.

b **Suggested answer**

I am writing in connection with my recent stay at your hotel. I have to say that I was not at all satisfied with the service provided.

8 Think about your conclusion

a The writer summarises feelings about the complaint, and asks for action to be taken, i.e. a refund, an explanation, etc.

9 Think about vocabulary

a **1** dissatisfied; **2** disappointed; **3** appalled, disgusted, furious; **4** annoyed, irritated; **5** inconvenienced; **6** furious; **7** taken aback; **8** put out; **9** fed up

b **Suggested answers**

1 appalling; **2** disgusting; **3** annoying; **4** irritated; **5** appalled; **6** disappointing

10 Think about grammar

a - You will stay in top-class hotels

   - All hotels are near the city centre

   - A sightseeing tour with a tourist guide is provided in every location

b The verb form is 'would be provided'. This verb form is used because the phrase is reporting what was originally said. The verb must shift back one tense in time.

c Reported speech answers are suggested below. Each one should be followed by a suitable complaint.

   Suggested answers

- Your advertisement stated that we could see the sights of the city, but ...

- You said that tours left at 8.30 a.m. every day, ...

- You claimed that all your guides spoke good English, French and Italian, ...

- Your advertisement stated that your guides were very knowledgeable ...

- You stated that all tours included the price of lunch in a traditional restaurant ...

Stories

 Describing an accident

1 Read the question

b

2 Think about your reader

1 a; **2** b

4 Read a model text

c c, e, f, b, d, a

d *Paragraph 1 – Introduction*
Question to readers, sentence which indicates a following narrative

Paragraph 2 – Situation before the accident
cold winter's day, new flat, boxes everywhere, felt cold, switched on heating

Paragraph 3 – How it happened
one hour later, heaters cold, turned knob, water everywhere, managed to stop the water

Paragraph 4 – How it ended
mopping up water, water in all the boxes.

Paragraph 5 – Conclusion
lesson – plumbing for experts

5 Think about your introduction

a By asking a question to arouse curiosity

b Good opening sentences are: 2, 3, 5

6 Think about vocabulary

a **1** bitterly cold, chilly, stone cold; **2** fiddling; **3** a fountain; **4** gushed; **5** soaking me to the skin; **6** gasped

b **Suggested answers**
Encourage the use of a dictionary (preferably a production dictionary such as the *Longman Language Activator* or the *Longman Essential Activator*.)

1 gorgeous/boiling hot/splendid

2 freezing/ chilly/fresh/ + invigorating/refreshing

3 hobbled/staggered

4 staring/glaring/leering

5 screamed/shouted/yelled

6 boiling hot/baking hot/intense

7 spotted/noticed/caught sight of/made out

8 leapt/jumped/sprang + sprinted/ dashed/rushed

7 Think about grammar

a All tenses refer to the past.

b *Underline*:
was arranging, began, managed, stopped, spent, had soaked

c The prompt words are to stimulate students to write a story, and should not be taken as obligatory. Students can change, add or delete words to write the story. A possible beginning of the story is suggested here if students find it hard to get started:

Suggested answer
One day last summer, I had a frightening experience. I was walking up a beautiful mountain trail, enjoying the sounds of the birds in the trees. This part of the trail was in a pine forest, and as I was walking, I noticed the sun had disappeared behind a black cloud.

Stories

Describing an event

1 Read the question

1 What happened? Who came?

2 b

3 Past simple, Past continuous, Past perfect

2 Think about your reader

1 Your pen friend

2 informal, chatty

3 Think about vocabulary

a *People who might be at a wedding*:
bride, bridegroom, best man, bridesmaids, priest, family, relatives, congregation, photographer, etc.

b **1** walks up the aisle; **2** gives away the bride; **3** performs the ceremony; **4** been exchanged; **5** blesses; **6** sign the register; **7** throw confetti; **8** have photographs taken; **9** reception is being held; **10** leave for their honeymoon

c Open-ended question. Encourage students to think about weddings they have been to, and how people reacted. Then ask them to select a word from the list 1–6 for each person they are thinking of. If they don't know the words, you can mime some of them, or ask students to look up the words in a dictionary, such as the *Longman Dictionary of Contemporary English*.

5 Compare two model texts

a Letter A

b **1** Description: Letter B, Narrative: Letter A

2 Letter A

3 Letter A

4 Letter B

c **2** Describing the people waiting in the church

3 Feelings and reactions as bride was late. What finally happened

4 What happened after the ceremony

6 Think about grammar

a *First example*: 'who' refers to the groom. Main verb is 'looked'.

Second example: 'who' refers to the priest. Main verb is 'was'.

b The sentences can be combined in different ways, as is shown in **1** below. All other sentences show one suggestion.

Suggested answers

1 The children, who were excited, were running around the church. OR:
The children, who were running around the church, were excited.

2 The bride's mother, who was looking upset, was dabbing her eyes with a tissue.

3 The best man, who was wearing a rose in his jacket, was talking to the groom.

4 The church, which was decorated with flowers, was looking beautiful.

c There are many ways to combine sentences here. Accept anything that makes sense. Get students to see that not every sentence should contain a non-defining clause, as overdoing it makes the writing look ridiculous.

Suggested answer

The bride, who was wearing a white silk dress and carrying a bouquet of white roses, was looking absolutely radiant. Two small children, who were about 5 years old and very sweet, were walking behind her, carrying the train of the bride's dress. They were wearing frilly white dresses. The bride's father, who was walking beside the bride and holding her arm, was looking very proud. He turned to the guests and beamed.

Stories
 A journey

2 Think about your reader

1 The judges of the competition

2 a, d, e, and possibly a short description of b, c, f. The main point is to narrate a story.

4 Think about vocabulary

Weather conditions: blizzard, downpour, fog, gale-force winds, icy conditions, snowstorm, thunder and lightning, heatwave, treacherous conditions

Effects of bad weather: communications cut off, delays, flooded streets, hold-ups, poor visibility, slippery roads, people get seasick, people get heat-stroke, people get stranded, roads blocked by fallen trees, ships pitch and roll, traffic grinds to a halt, vehicles skid, choppy sea

Adjectives: chilly, freezing, humid, stifling, sweltering

5 Read a model text

a 3

b *Paragraph 1*: Background, where, who when, why travelling
Paragraph 2: Start of the storm, lounge scene,
Paragraph 3: End of the journey, didn't enjoy holiday

6 Think about your introduction

a 1 The family of the writer, and the writer

2 To Ireland

3 A few years ago

4 They were going on holiday

5 By ferry

6 Stormy

b **Suggested answer**

One day last week, some of my friends and I decided to go on a day trip out of the city to a beautiful village up in the mountains. We were all tired after working all week, and were looking forward to a pleasant relaxing time in the warm, late autumn weather. We didn't realise then that we would have completely the opposite experience.

7 Think about tenses

b 1 thought; 2 had arrived; 3 assumed; 4 had been delayed; 5 would turn up; 6 noticed; 7 had disappeared; 8 was; 9 would get; 10 looked

8 Think about connectors

a *Underline*:
despite, although

b 1 Wrong. Despite the traffic jam, …

2 Wrong. Although I had packed my suitcase carefully, I forgot my toothbrush.

3 Correct

4 Correct

5 Wrong. Despite her heavy suitcase, … OR: Although her suitcase was heavy, …

6 Wrong. Despite the heavy rain … OR: Although the rain was heavy, …

c 1 Despite the dry weather, the country still looked green.
Although the weather was dry, the country still looked green.

2 Despite his exhaustion, he finished the race.
Although he was exhausted, he finished the race.

3 Despite the high waves, I went swimming.
Although the waves were high, I went swimming.

4 Despite the rain, we went to the park.
Although it was raining, we went to the park.

5 Despite her illness, Liza didn't go to bed.
Although Liza was ill, she didn't go to bed.

Stories
A story beginning

2 Think about your reader

1 In the exam, a magazine may not be specified. In this case, get students to decide what kind of magazine it is, so that they can write more easily with a target reader in mind.

2 b

3 Think about vocabulary

b 1 had rehearsed/had been rehearsing; 2 dimmed; 3 minor role/part … lines; 4 the leading role; 5 piece of music; 6 took a bow; 7 standing ovation; 8 scenery … props; 9 stage fright; 10 clapped and cheered

5 Read a model text

a a mixture of positive and negative

b **Suggested answers**

Start paragraph 2 with 'I took a deep breath …'

Start paragraph 3 with: 'At last, it was all over …'

6 Link your text

a *Underline*:

In a few minutes, At first, gradually, Soon, At last,

b *Start of the story*: At first

Events that happened slowly: gradually

Events in the future of the story: In a few minutes, Soon

End of the story: At last

Elicit other words that the students know, to fill in the table. Check answers in the **Writing bank**, *FC Writing* Students' Book, page 128.

7 Think about tenses

a *Underline*:

am (afraid), will fall down, think, will laugh, am sure, will forget, am terrified, am going to make, think, will drop, am scared, won't be, am worried, won't clap, am positive, will disappoint

b **1** I was afraid I would fall down on the stage.

2 I thought that everyone would laugh at me.

3 I was sure that I would forget my part.

4 I was terrified that I was going to make a mistake.

5 I thought I would drop my violin.

6 I was scared that I wouldn't be very good.

7 I was worried that the audience wouldn't clap at the end.

8 I was positive that I would disappoint my audience.

Stories

 A story ending

2 Think about your reader

1 Your teacher, and the students who read the magazine

2 Fairly informal

4 Think about paragraphing

a The text is written with very short, simple sentences, no linking words, and no paragraphing.

b **Suggested answers**

Paragraph 2 starts: 'Naturally, she panicked.'

Paragraph 3 starts: 'Marianna suggested…'

c There are almost an infinite number of ways to combine the sentences. Revise different ways to combine sentences, with different linking words, relative clauses, etc., that the students have already met in the book so far. Encourage students to be concise by making reduced clauses too.

---

d If students need some guidance, ask them to look at certain places in the story: when she looked in her bag, when they failed to find the wallet, when Marianna suggested that they went to the police, for example.

5 Think about punctuation

1 'Please show me what you have in a size 10,' she asked.

2 'Can I try this on?' she asked.

3 She said, 'This is too big. Have you got a smaller size?'

4 She screamed, 'My wallet's been stolen!'

5 'What does your wallet look like?' asked the manager.

6 'It's brown leather with a black zip,' she said.

6 Think about vocabulary

Happy: delighted, elated, overjoyed, thrilled

Sad: dejected, despondent, distraught, downhearted

Exciting: exhilarated, thrilled

Frightening: petrified, scared stiff, terrified

7 Edit your text

a **Error correction examples**

I <u>did</u> my homework.

I was very <u>interested</u> in the book.

I am <u>writing</u> to you …

<u>I'm</u> leaving tomorrow.

I <u>saw</u> him last week.

He likes chocolate <u>very much</u>.

When I <u>finish</u>, I'll call you.

I love listening <u>to</u> music.

b One day, I decided <u>to take</u> my youngest sister to the circus. My sister was very <u>excited</u>, and she couldn't wait in the queue to buy our tickets. She <u>told</u> me, 'John, I am going inside.' 'Wait! You <u>can't go</u> in without a ticket!' I replied, but she didn't <u>hear</u> me. When I <u>had bought</u> the tickets, I thought that my sister <u>would</u> be waiting <u>for</u> me at the entrance of the circus. I was wrong. I asked the man at the door, '<u>Have you</u> seen a little girl?' He said, 'A little girl ran past me and went inside.' I thanked him, and <u>went</u> inside to start looking for her. The show <u>hadn't started</u> yet, and I couldn't find her, <u>although</u> I <u>looked</u> everywhere, even under the chairs. After a while, I remembered that she <u>loved animals</u>, and that when she <u>grew</u> up, she <u>wanted</u> to become <u>a</u> vet. So I thought that she might be with the animals at the back of the circus. I was very <u>relieved</u> when I saw her <u>laughing</u> with the monkeys …

8 Think about grammar

a **1** told, offered

b *Put a tick beside*: explain, say, suggest

Write 1 beside: advise, agree, ask, encourage, offer, promise, refuse, warn, tell

Write G beside: admit, accuse, apologise, deny,

Verbs needing prepositions: accuse someone **of**, apologise **for**, explain something **to** someone

c **1** I accused the sales assistant of stealing my money.

2 The sales assistant denied stealing my money.

3 Marianna advised me to go to the police.

4 Marianna suggested that I looked in the plastic bag.

5 The sales assistant admitted stealing my money.

6 Jane refused to do it.

7 Marianna apologised for not keeping an eye on my bag.

8 My father warned me never to leave my bag open again.

Discursive compositions

Discussing pros and cons

2 Think about your reader

1 Your teacher; **2** b; **3** c; **4** b

4 Read a model text

Main topic	Topic Sentences	Details
2 Pros	Exams can indeed have beneficial results.	revision, preparation for real life stress
3 Cons	On the other hand, exams can have negative effects.	problems of stress, not the best way to find a student's ability, facts quickly forgotten

5 Think about your introduction and conclusion

a 2

b 3

c Students may need to discuss the topics first, as they will write the two main paragraphs in **6 Think about connectors** below.

6 Think about connectors

a **1** However, On the other hand,

2 In addition, another ...

3 As a result, consequently, This in turn,

b The students already have some ideas, and an introduction and conclusion for the topics. Ask students to choose one of them, and make an outline of the main ideas for the two body paragraphs. This can be done in pairs or groups before writing. The final piece of writing will include the introduction and conclusion prepared in **5c**.

7 Think about grammar

a The article is used because the 'stressful situations' are described in detail with a relative clause, and are therefore specific, not general.

b As some of us know, experimenting on <u>animals</u> gives benefits to <u>humans</u>, but harms animals a great deal. Currently, <u>science</u> has made everything possible. By turning theory into reality, <u>scientists</u> have found useful cures for those patients who may have never had the chance of being healthy. For example, patients who had <u>cancer</u>, thanks to <u>new technology</u>, are healthy. Another great achievement is in the treatment of <u>hereditary</u> <u>diseases</u>. Cures have been found after <u>scientists</u> located the genes which cause them. Such efforts are also being made for <u>diabetes</u> and <u>obesity</u>. At the same time, while people are being cured, many animals are suffering in <u>laboratories</u>. Just because <u>man</u> is more important than <u>animals</u>, it doesn't mean we can do whatever we like.

Discursive compositions

Giving your opinion 1

2 Think about your reader

1 Your teacher

2 fairly formal

3 text with no special format

4 a, b, c, d, g, and possibly h, if students can't make a decision one way or another. (See **tip**, page 80.)

3 Think about vocabulary

School subjects

a **1** Physics, Chemistry and Biology

2 Many possible answers: athletics, gymnastics, various sports, etc.

3 Home Economics: cooking, sewing; Design Technology: study of design of products, furniture, etc., with the practical skills of technical drawing, and making articles; Information Technology: computer studies

4 Possible answers: Art, Drama, English, French, German, Greek, History, Latin, Music, Religious Studies, Geography

b **1** Maths is difficult

2 French is easy.

Practical Skills

Other possible ideas: learning how to drive, open a bank account, time management skills, study skills for college, learning about living away from home, job interview skills, etc.

5 Read a model text

1 The writer agrees. *Underline*: 'I couldn't agree more ...'

2 paragraph 2 – job interview skills; paragraph 3 – domestic skills; paragraph 4 – money management skills.

3 By making a hypothetical statement, speculating about the consequences.

6 Think about paragraphing

a *Red*: One important skill schools should teach is how to succeed in a job interview.

Blue: so that school leavers can feel confident …

Black: My first job interview only exposed my inadequacies, and I failed to get the job.

b *Paragraph 3*:

Red: Boys as well as girls should be taught how to cook and sew.

Blue: As a result, young people will not suffer the shock of coping alone when they leave home.

Black: I, for example, was grateful for my Home Economics lessons during my first weeks at university.

Paragraph 4:

Red: Another important skill is learning how to manage money…

Blue: … so that young people don't spend their grant or salary all at once.

Black: My first pay cheque disappeared in only one week, and I immediately had to borrow. Consequently, I was always trying to repay my debts.

7 Link your text

a *Underline*:

so that, As a result, consequently

b Any answers expressing a result should be accepted. Discuss a variety of possible results with the class first, if you think they need help with ideas.

8 Think about language

a *Underline*:

1 I completely agree; **2** I believe …; **3** In my opinion, …; **4** I strongly disagree …; **5** I think …; **6** As far as I am concerned …; **7** In my view …

b *Strong agreement*: 1, 3

Strong disagreement: 5, 6

Partial: 2, 4, 7

c Get students to discuss ideas in pairs, then they can complete the exercise expressing their own feelings on the subject.

Discursive compositions

19 Giving your opinion 2

1 Read the question

a Expresses the meaning of the statement

2 Think about your reader

1 Your teacher

2 fairly formal

3 no special format needed

3 Think about vocabulary

Sports and outdoor activities

go: bowling, cycling, fishing, parachuting, sailing, skating, swimming, snowboarding, windsurfing

do: athletics, gymnastics, outdoor activities, sports

play: basketball, hockey, volleyball, football

Benefits of leisure activities

Suggested answers:

improve circulation: S

improve hand/eye co-ordination: S, CG

increase mental alertness: S, CG, (TV)

help cope with stress: S, CG, TV

provide an outlet for excess energy: S

develop social skills: S

build team spirit: S

give access to information: CG, TV

broaden education: CG, TV

improve problem-solving skills: (S), CG

increase awareness of the world: TV, (CG)

provide a break from studying: S, CG, TV

5 Read a model text

a **1** the writer partly agrees.
Underline: ' I agree with the statement to a certain extent …'

2 Yes

3 The introduction states the writer's opinion, and outlines the main points that the essay will discuss. The conclusion suggests the need for balance in our lives.

b **1** Introduction stating position on the topic

2 Benefits of TV

3 Benefits of computer games

4 Conclusion, stating the need for balance

c The students should be encouraged to look for a number of different ways to fill each gap, in pairs or groups. Then each student can choose which idea they like the best to complete the exercise.

Suggested answers

I completely disagree with the statement. Many young people today have too <u>much to do in their busy school life</u>, so TV and computer games are a good way <u>to get a break from studying</u>. Computer games and TV programmes offer many benefits. One important example is <u>a computer game which tests your intelligence</u>. For example, I saw a computer game where <u>the player had to solve maths puzzles in order to get points</u>. In addition to the benefits offered by computer games, TV has its advantages, too. Many programmes are <u>educational</u>, such as <u>documentaries on wildlife, travel, and history</u>. As far as I am concerned, young people should spend their leisure time <u>playing computer games and watching TV, to relieve them from stress</u>. This means that they will <u>be able to cope with their daily life better</u>. In addition, they can <u>learn and relax at the same time</u>. Parents should also <u>encourage this, not forbid it</u>.

6 Think about paragraphing

a No

b This is a more complex task for students to handle, and should be guided. A procedure could be as follows:

1 First ask students to underline all the information about TV, then about computer games, in two different colour pens.

2 Students then make notes of the ideas on a separate piece of paper, and put them in a logical order.

3 Students then think about how they can link these organised ideas together with suitable connecting words.

4 When the two main paragraphs have been organised, students will need to decide which paragraph comes first and second.

5 The introduction and conclusion are reasonable, but students could revise these too, if they wish.

7 Link your text

a *Underline*:

For example, such as, For instance, One example of ... is ...

b Students can discuss possible examples in pairs, before completing the exercise. Encourage students to name actual examples that they have personal experience of. It is important to make the examples highly specific.

Discursive compositions
20 Suggesting solutions

1 Read the question

1 What do you think is the best way for them to do this?

2 What can ordinary people do to protect endangered species?

2 Think about your reader

1 Your teacher

2 fairly formal

3 no special format needed

3 Think about vocabulary

a **1** extinction; **2** dying; **3** extinct

b *Hunting*: fur, ivory, over-fishing, skins, whale oil

Threats to habitat: farming, forest clearance, housing, mining, motorways

Pollution: industrial waste, mining, motorways, sewerage

c **1** join; **2** donate; **3** charities; **4** lobby; **5** laws; **6** ban

5 Compare two model texts

a *Writing checklist*

- Text 1 does not write about the 'best way', but simply lists possibilities that ordinary people can do. Text 2 covers the key points well.

- Text 1 has a paragraphing problem, Text 2 is well organised.

- Text 1 Has a general introductory sentence, but clear topic sentences are missing. Text 2 has clear text signals through the use of topic sentences.

- Text 1 uses connectors within sentences, but does not use linking words to show the logical connection *between* sentences. Text 2 has a good level of cohesion through the use of connectors and linking words.

- Both texts do this, but Text 2 does it better.

- Text 1 has a paragraph which looks like a conclusion, ('Children are the future ... if we do not do something now.') but it is not at the end! This gives a personal comment. Text 2 both summarises and includes a personal comment

b See Unit 19, **6 Think about paragraphing, b**, for a guided procedure for revising an essay.

6 Think about your introduction

a **1** 'It is one of the great disasters of this century ... land clearance.'

   2 'I believe that ordinary people ... endangered species.'

b Encourage students to think about forms of transport that they know. They can identify those that cause pollution, and those that don't. Discuss with the class what background sentence would help to familiarise the reader with the topic, perhaps mentioning all forms of transport, and what some of them do to the environment. The next sentence should focus on the main point of the question, and students can choose which forms of transport they wish to write about.

7 Edit your text

a **Corrections**

Many people <u>think</u> that the problem of protecting the environment is <u>the</u> concern of the government, but I believe that ordinary people can do <u>something</u> too. I think that we can give money to a charity <u>that</u> (delete 'it') <u>protects</u> the <u>environment</u>. Our donations can help to change things, however small <u>they</u> may be. In addition, we must stop killing wild animals and <u>destroying</u> (delete 'the') <u>nature</u>. We can join a local organisation and take part in <u>its</u> activities. Furthermore, there are many other problems that we must <u>solve</u> (delete 'them'). People can help reduce pollution by walking or taking the bus to work everyday instead of <u>driving</u> their cars. <u>Apart from</u> this, we can try to drive only when it is absolutely necessary. We should all try to protect the environment, because if we continue to damage the Earth, our children <u>won't have anywhere</u> to live.

b This exercise is designed to improve the variety and complexity of sentence structure. Choose three or four examples of sentences that can be revised, or sentences that can be combined, using co-ordinate or subordinate clauses. When students understand the nature of the task, they can work on the whole text in pairs/groups. Groups could write their version on an overhead transparency, if available, and each group version could be discussed and evaluated. The same thing can be done by photocopying the revisions.

Reports

21 Evaluating places

2 Think about your reader
1 Your boss; **2** Formal; **3** b, e; **4** a

a and c are not <u>new</u> attractions; d is not a tourist attraction.

4 Think about format and style
Number 2 is a report; the headings, and formal, impersonal language are the main features that characterise a report.

5 Think about vocabulary
1 Payment is made on arrival.
2 Drinks are available at the bar.
3 The club is located just before the Grand Hotel.
4 The entrance fee is £5.
5 The club would appeal to many people.
6 I would strongly recommend this place.
7 It is within easy reach of town.
8 Reduced rates are available for groups.

6 Read a model text
1 Yes; **2** Yes; **3** Yes, due to the format used, information is easily found under headings, and key points stand out through the use of numbers. Sentences are concise, and simple in structure, so that information words are easily read.

7 Make a plan
1 Introductory sentence similar to the one in the model text in **6**.
2 Entrance fee, Right in the city centre, Opening times.
3 Cafeteria, shop, lift and wheelchair access.
4 Commentary in a variety of languages.
5 Each period of history clearly divided into rooms, clear and well-presented displays.
6 Not open at weekends, A lot to see in one day, can be tiring.
7 Students should think if the advantages outweigh the negative points, or vice versa, and write a suitable recommendation, following the model text in **6**.

8 Think about your introduction
a Number 2 is better, as it is written in an impersonal, formal style. Number 1 is too general in its opening sentence, and does not outline the purpose of the report.

b Students should write a similar introductory sentence as in the model text in **6**.

9 Think about your conclusion
a The purpose of the conclusion is to make a recommendation.

b The conclusion is not suitable, as it does not recommend the suitability of the attraction for foreign tourists.

10 Think about grammar
a *Underline*:
can be reached, can be hired, is not cleaned.

b **1** The toilets are not kept clean.
2 A different buffet lunch is served every day.
3 The beach is not cleaned, so rubbish can be seen everywhere.
4 All visitors are made to feel welcome.
5 Tourists guides are provided.

Reports

22 Evaluating proposals

2 Think about your reader
1 c

2 A member or members of the town council will read the report. They are very busy people, who need to read information presented in a clear format, where the main points are easy to find, and where the language is simple and concise.

3 Formal and impersonal.

4 Report format is needed, with a memo-style heading, and headings and numbering in the main body of the report.

4 Read a model text
a Suggested answers
Introduction
Benefits of a stadium
Benefits of a theatre
Conclusion/Recommendation

b 1 Yes; **2** Yes; **3** The conclusion recommends the better of the two projects, and gives reasons for this choice.

5 Think about paragraphing
a **1** *Introduction*
purpose – recommend which project would benefit the town

2 *Stadium*
top-class competitions

3 *Theatre*
operas, plays, cinema
venue for local events – school concerts, dance festival

4 *Conclusion*
recommendation sports stadium, more facilities for more people, jobs

6 Think about vocabulary
b **1** do; **2** make; **3** be done/do; **4** make; **5** do;
6 make; **7** making; **8** make

7 Think about grammar
a The verb form used is the second conditional.

b Get students to discuss what possible benefits there

HH LEARNING CENTRE
HARROW COLLEGE

are, and then to write their sentences. Although this is the second conditional, the 'if' clause is only needed for the first sentence. All the following sentences should have the 'would do' form of the verb.

Reports
23 Suggesting improvements

2 Think about your reader
1 The museum director
2 e, with the possibility of a and c as supporting details. b and d do not refer to children.

4 Edit your text
a This exercise helps students to revise writing according to the teacher's comments. Suggested revisions are given, but accept anything that has attempted to deal with the comments:

Introduction: The purpose of this report is to recommend ways to make the museum more interesting to young children.

1 Activity leaflets could be given to children.
2 Point 2 is really part of point 1, so the text would be best if it was renumbered throughout. The underlined sentence should be put in the previous paragraph, and joined with a linking word: 'In addition, pictures of the exhibits could be given to children, which could be coloured in according to what the exhibits look like.'
4 A museum guide, who knows how to stimulate children's interest, could be employed.
5 This point is irrelevant material and should be deleted. Students should add another suggestion, which can be taken from **3 Brainstorm the topic**.

Heading suggested: Conclusion

b 1 Yes; 2 Point 5 is not a suggestion, and is not relevant; 3 Yes; 4 Yes; 5 Yes. The report is about 160 words.

Train students to calculate roughly how many words they write, as in the **exam tip** box. Encourage your classes to write compositions close to the upper word limit, rather than the lower.

5 Think about vocabulary
1 popularity; 2 exhibition; 3 variety; 4 attraction; 5 scientific; 6 understanding; 7 curiosity; 8 creativity

6 Think about language
a *Underline*:

could be given, would be, could play, would be

b The topics given in the question may need some pair or group discussion before students write their suggestions. Check the answers contain the conditional form of the verb.

Articles
24 Describing people & relationships

2 Think about your reader
1 a, d
2 *Tick*:

a, b, d, e, f, g, are the most suitable.

The main part of the article should be concerned with f and g.

Options for brief background information, probably in the introduction could be: a, d, e.

Short anecdotes (option b) could be included as illustrations of main points in the main paragraphs.

Options c and h are not relevant.

4 Read a model text
a 1 Yes; 2 Yes; 3 Yes
b 1 Introduction, background information
  2 His role as a basketball player
  3 His role in business
  4 Conclusion, summarising the main points.

5 Make a plan
The plan suggested below is one possible version. Students may decide to order the details and paragraphs differently.

First, identify background details suitable for an introduction. (Born 1910, Albania, nun from age of 18, India, Famous for helping the poor in India)

The second paragraph could contain information about her work (Saw sick people on Calcutta streets, started order)

Paragraph 3 could contain a description of her character, lifestyle and devotion.

Paragraph 4 Conclusion – Nobel Prize, description of her funeral. This paragraph should also make it clear why she is important enough to be included in this book.

6 Think about vocabulary
a 1 influenced; 2 admiration; 3 creative; 4 realised, ambition; 5 discoveries; 6 inventor; 7 devoted; 8 founded; 9 pioneer
b

Noun	Verb	Adjective	Person
influence	influence	influential	
admiration	admire	admirable	admirer
creation	create	creative	creator
ambition		ambitious	
achievement	achieve		achiever
devotion	devote	devoted	
invention	invent	inventive	inventor
discovery	discover		discoverer

7 Think about connectors
a *Underline*:

because, as, due to, since

b Encourage students to get practice in using all the connectors in **a**. Some discussion to get ideas might be needed before the students write.